W9-BVU-372

10/2/06

www.sugargrove.lib.il.us

Rookie
Read-About® Math

Giraffe Graphs

By Melissa Stewart

Subject Consultant
Robyn Silbey
Math Content Coach
Montgomery County Public Schools
Maryland

Reading Consultant
Cecilia Minden-Cupp, PhD
Former Director, Language and Literacy Program
Harvard Graduate School of Education

Children's Press®
A Division of Scholastic Inc.
New York   Toronto   London   Auckland   Sydney
Mexico City   New Delhi   Hong Kong
Danbury, Connecticut

Special thanks to the San Francisco Zoological Society
for the use of their location for photographing
several of the images for this book.

Designer: Herman Adler
Photo Researcher: Caroline Anderson
The photo on the cover shows a giraffe.

Library of Congress Cataloging-in-Publication Data

Stewart, Melissa.
  Giraffe graphs / by Melissa Stewart.
    p. cm. — (Rookie read-about math)
  Includes index.
  ISBN-10: 0-516-23798-5 (lib. bdg.)   0-516-24594-5 (pbk.)
  ISBN-13: 978-0-516-23798-5 (lib. bdg.)   978-0-516-24594-2 (pbk.)
  1. Graph theory—Juvenile literature. I. Title. II. Series.
  QA166.S74 2006
  511'.5—dc22   2005032731

CHILDREN'S PRESS, and ROOKIE READ-ABOUT®,
and associated logos are trademarks and/or registered trademarks
of Scholastic Library Publishing. SCHOLASTIC and associated logos
are trademarks and/or registered trademarks of Scholastic Inc.

1 2 3 4 5 6 7 8 9 10 R 16 15 14 13 12 11 10 09 08 07

Have you ever been to a zoo? I have. My class went to the zoo on a field trip.

My teacher says that a picture is worth a thousand words. That means one quick look at a picture can tell you a lot.

I took a picture of some of the kids in my group at the zoo. Make a list of everything this picture tells you.

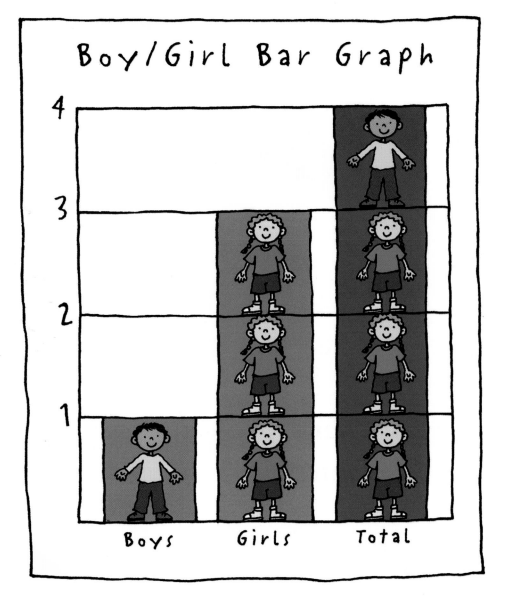

6

My teacher also says that a graph is worth a thousand numbers. One quick look at a graph can tell you a lot, too.

Here is a bar graph of the kids in my picture. How many boys are in the picture? How many girls are in the picture?

My group liked visiting the giraffes.

Animal Tally Chart

Giraffes

We used a tally chart to keep track of how many animals we saw. We did this by making a mark for each animal we counted.

This tally chart shows how many giraffes we saw in the giraffe exhibit.

After we saw the giraffes, we went to the elephant exhibit. Now our tally chart shows how many giraffes and how many elephants we saw.

Animal Tally Chart

Giraffes

Elephants

Animal Tally Chart

Giraffes

Elephants

Lions

Next, we saw the lions. We added the number of lions we saw to our tally sheets, too.

When we got back to school, we made a bar graph comparing how many giraffes, elephants, and lions we saw.

Take a look. Which animal did we see the most?

17

When we were at the zoo,
we started thinking about how
tall the giraffes were compared
to the other animals.

Our teacher helped us look up the height of giraffes without their necks and heads. This is called shoulder height. It's a measurement used to compare animals.

Then we looked up the shoulder height for elephants and lions.

We drew a bar graph to help us compare the shoulder height of the three animals. Which animal is the tallest?

If you said "giraffes," you are correct!

Next, my teacher asked us to vote for our favorite animal. I voted for the giraffe. I think giraffes are cute!

This bar graph shows the results of our "favorite animal" vote.

Which animal got the most votes? How can you tell by reading the bar graph?

Tally charts and bar graphs helped us learn a lot today. Sometimes, drawing a picture of our numbers makes it easier to find the answer to a question.

When I go home, I'm going to look for graphs in magazines and in the newspaper.

Why don't you look for some graphs, too?

Words You Know

bar graph

elephants

giraffes

lions

tally chart

zoo

Index

About the Author

Award-winning author Melissa Stewart has written more than sixty books for children and is a frequent contributor to Scholastic Inc.'s MATH magazine.

Photo Credits

All photographs © 2007 Richard Hutchings Photography.
Illustrations by Patrick Girouard.